A HISTORICAL ALBUM OF

ILLINOIS

A HISTORICAL ALBUM OF

ILLINOIS

Charles A. Wills

THE MILLBROOK PRESS, Brookfield, Connecticut

Front and back cover: "View of Rush Street Bridge," colored lithograph by Charles Shober, after E. Whitfield, Chicago, 1861. Library of Congress.

Title page: Farm scene, western Illinois. Courtesy of the Illinois Information Service.

Library of Congress Cataloguing-in-Publication Data

Wills, Charles.
    A historical album of Illinois / Charles A. Wills.
        p. cm. — (Historical albums)
    Includes bibliographical references and index.
    Summary: A history of Illinois, highlighting the contrasts of the state
(both as an agricultural and industrial center).
    ISBN 1-56294-482-7 (lib. bdg.)   ISBN 1-56294-761-3 (pbk.)
    1. Illinois—History—Juvenile literature. 2. Illinois—Gazetteers—Juvenile
literature. [1. Illinois—History]
I. Title. II. Series.
F541.3.W55 1994
977.3—dc20   93-35017
                                                        CIP
                                                          AC

Created in association with Media Projects Incorporated

    C. Carter Smith, *Executive Editor*
    Lelia Wardwell, *Managing Editor*
    Charles A. Wills, *Principal Writer*
    Bernard Schleifer, *Art Director*
    Shelley Latham, *Production Editor*
    Arlene Goldberg, *Cartographer*

    Consultant: Frederick Drake, Department of History,
Illinois State University, Normal, Illinois

CONTENTS

Introduction

One of the first European explorers to visit the land that became the state of Illinois described what he saw: "A vast ocean of meadowland, in some parts . . . dotted with coasts, capes or islands of forest-wood." The explorer was describing the prairies—the rolling grasslands that once covered much of Illinois. The fertile prairie soil was what attracted the pioneers who settled the region, so Illinois has long been known as "the Prairie State."

A better nickname for Illinois might be "the Crossroads State." Located in the middle of North America, bordered by the Great Lakes and the Mississippi River, Illinois is a place where north and south, east and west meet. The region was a crossroads for Native American traders long before the first white people arrived in the 1600s. In the 19th century, the state's greatest city, Chicago, became the transportation hub of the nation. Even today, if you fly from New York to California or vice versa, there's a good chance you'll go by way of Chicago.

Modern Illinois is a state of contrasts. Chicago is as far north as Boston, Massachusetts; Cairo, in southern Illinois, is as far south as Richmond, Virginia. In Illinois, you can hear a dozen languages spoken on a bustling Chicago street, or listen to the wind rustle the stalks in a quiet "downstate" cornfield. It is a state with a long and rich history, filled with interesting and diverse people—farmers and physicists, politicians and poets, presidents and gangsters. Together, Illinois's history and geography make it one of the nation's most interesting and important states.

THE PRAIRIE STATE

Farmers harvest hay on an Illinois prairie farm in this 19th-century lithograph. Today, Illinois ranks fourth among all states in agricultural wealth.

The land we know as Illinois was once home to remarkable Native American civilizations. Later, its forests and prairies were the territory of the Illiniwek people, who welcomed the first Europeans in the region—French explorers, missionaries, and traders—in the late 1600s. First claimed by France, then by Britain, the Illinois country became part of the United States during the Revolutionary War. Winning statehood in 1818, Illinois quickly became the destination of thousands of pioneers, who were attracted by its fertile land. By the middle of the 19th century, Illinois had become one of the nation's leading states.

The Early People of Illinois

In the distant past, glaciers—huge, slow-moving rivers of ice—covered almost all of what is now Illinois. About 10,000 years ago, the glaciers slowly retreated north, leaving behind vast stretches of flat land covered with tall grasses. These flatlands, or prairies, once covered more than half of the present state of Illinois. But although Illinois is called the Prairie State, much of northern Illinois was heavily forested. Trees lined the banks of the more than 500 rivers and streams that crisscrossed the region.

Native Americans arrived in Illinois not long after the glaciers melted. They lived by hunting game and gathering wild plants. Over the centuries, a flourishing Native American civilization, the Hopewell culture, developed in the Midwest, including Illinois. The Hopewell people practiced farming and buried their dead in raised mounds of earth. Around AD 500 the Hopewell people died out, for reasons still unknown.

Three centuries later, a new and remarkable culture, the Mississippian, arose in Illinois and the surrounding areas. Like the Hopewell people, the Mississippians built mounds, but they used mounds as temples for religious ceremonies in addition to burial sites. About 10,000 surviving mounds still dot Illinois's landscape. The largest,

This is an artist's re-creation of the great Cahokia mound built by the Mississippian people. The earthworks were built primarily for burials, but sometimes developed into plazas with temples and civic centers.

Monk's Mound near present-day East St. Louis, is 100 feet high and covers seventeen acres. Scholars believe as many as 100,000 people lived in a city surrounding the mound. The Mississippian people were traders and travelers as well as great builders. They may have been in contact with places as far away as Mexico, and Mississippian pottery has been found in Florida.

By 1500, the Mississippian culture had fallen into a decline and vanished. Because the Mississippians never developed writing, there are no records to tell us what happened to them. The Mississippian population may have grown faster than its food supply, leading to starvation. Some scientists think that diseases brought by early European explorers spread to Illinois and wiped out the Mississippian culture.

Just after the disappearance of the Mississippians, Illinois became home to a group of Native American tribes who spoke the Algonquian language. These people called themselves Illiniwek, meaning "the superior men." The Illiniweks planted corn and squash on the prairies and hunted buffalo and other game. For about a century, the Illiniweks had the prairies and forests of Illinois to themselves. Then, in the mid-1600s, terrifying newcomers from the East began to appear in Illinois.

Many artifacts have been uncovered from the mounds built by people who lived in Illinois thousands of years ago, like the gorget (protective throat cover) with a spider design (top) and the ceramic bowl shaped like a bird (above). The Mississippian culture was well known for its pottery, which was often made in the shapes of humans, birds, and animals and painted white, red, brown, and black.

The Voyageurs

Traveling in birchbark canoes, hardy French-Canadian fur traders explored the rivers of North America. Five explorers went with Marquette and Jolliet on their 1673 expedition into the Illinois country.

The new arrivals were the Iroquois—Native Americans from a powerful league of tribes living in present-day New York State. By this time, European traders had reached Iroquois territory. The traders bought the fur of beavers and other animals, which they traded in Europe. In return, the Iroquois received guns, alcohol, and other goods

When fur-bearing animals became scarce in New York, Iroquois warriors moved west to find new sources of furs. Soon the Iroquois and Illiniweks were fighting for control of Illinois. The Illiniweks didn't have firearms, so they were no match for the well-armed Iroquois. Many Illiniweks died during long years of fighting.

As the power of the Illiniwek tribe declined, Native Americans from other parts of the Midwest—the Miami, Sauk and Fox, and Potawatomi tribes—came to Illinois. Weakened by disease and war, the Illiniweks could do little to defend their homeland.

The first Europeans reached Illinois not long after the Iroquois. In the 17th century, France took the lead in

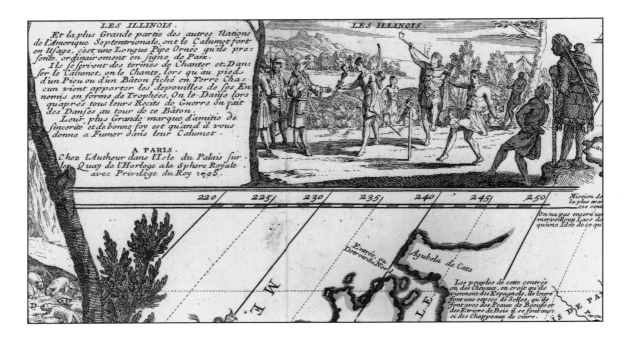

This detail from a 1705 map (above) shows Illiniweks offering the calumet (peace pipe) to a group of French explorers. By this time, other Native American peoples had driven the Illiniweks from most of their traditional lands.

Born in France, Father Jacques Marquette came to Canada as a missionary in 1666. He spent six years living with the Ottawa Native Americans in Quebec before setting out on his explorations of Illinois and the Mississippi River. He is shown in this drawing (left) with some of the rivers he charted behind him.

exploring and settling Canada. From their outposts in Canada, French explorers, traders, and missionaries traveled south into the lands around the Great Lakes and the Mississippi River Valley, looking for furs to trade and Native Americans to convert to the Roman Catholic Church.

At some point, French *voyageurs*—fur traders—may have paddled their canoes into Illinois, but the first Europeans known to have reached the area were Father Jacques Marquette, a priest of the Jesuit religious order, and Louis Jolliet, a soldier.

Marquette, Jolliet, and five voyageurs left St. Ignace, Michigan, in May 1673. After a month of travel on the Wisconsin and Mississippi rivers, the party's birchbark canoes reached northeastern Illinois. After meeting a group of friendly Illiniweks, the explorers crossed Illinois from west to east by way of the Illinois and Des Plaines rivers.

Marquette and Jolliet saw that the region's open prairies were ideal for farming and settlement. In most other areas, a settler would have to spend years cutting down and burning trees to clear land. But in Illinois, Marquette observed, "On the very day of his arrival, he could put his plow into the ground."

The explorers also observed that the waterways of the Illinois country could provide France with a highway into the heart of North America. From Lake Michigan, voyageurs needed only to portage, or carry, their canoes a few miles to the Des Plaines River, which flowed into the Illinois River, which in turn connected to the great Mississippi. Marquette even predicted that one day a canal would be built between Lake Michigan and the Des Plaines River, making the portage unnecessary.

In 1674, Marquette returned to Illinois to found a religious mission, but he became ill and died in 1675. Jolliet never returned to Illinois. The task of exploring the region fell to another two-man team—Robert Cavalier, Sieur de la Salle, from France, and his assistant, Italian-born Henri de Tonti. In 1680, La Salle and Tonti built a crude fort near the site of present-day Peoria. The following year, the explorers paddled down the Mississippi from Illinois to the Gulf of Mexico. On the return trip upriver, La Salle built a larger post, Fort St. Louis, on a cliff overlooking the Illinois River.

None of the outposts built by La Salle and Tonti lasted more than a few years. Not until 1699 was there a permanent French settlement in Illinois—Cahokia, a mission founded by French Jesuits in the region known as "the American Bottom." Four years later, another settlement, Kaskaskia, was established nearby. Kaskaskia became the largest settlement in the Illinois country—the name the French gave to the land of the Illiniwek Indians.

The Struggle for Control

Missionaries, traders, and settlers arrived in Illinois in the first half of the 18th century. The fur trade was still important, and wheat from the farms around Kaskaskia helped feed other French settlements in the Mississippi Valley. Still, there were never more than 2,000 non-Indians in Illinois during the French era. This number included several hundred slaves brought upriver from New Orleans, which was founded by the French in 1719.

French rule over Illinois lasted less than a century. In 1756, France and the other major colonial power in North America, Great Britain, went to war over control of Canada. The conflict (known as the French and Indian War) ended with France's defeat in 1763. The French empire in Canada and the Mississippi Valley then came under British rule. A few English-speaking traders arrived in the region, but the British did little to develop the remote, sparsely settled Illinois country.

In 1775, thirteen of Britain's North American colonies began a war for independence. British forts on the Western frontier, including Kaskaskia and other posts in Illinois, began supplying Indians with weapons. Soon, Native Americans were raiding settlements in Kentucky, a region then claimed by Virginia.

George Rogers Clark, a young Virginia-born frontiersman, had a plan to stop the raids—and capture the Illinois country for Virginia. After gathering about 200 frontiersmen from settlements in Kentucky and along the Ohio River, Clark captured Kaskaskia on July 4, 1778. The victory meant little, however, because a British force soon occupied Vincennes, a major settlement in what is now Indiana.

Clark decided on a bold action. With 175 frontiersmen—nicknamed "Long Knives" because of the hunting weapons they carried—Clark left Kaskaskia in February 1779.

After a brutal eighteen-day march through 140 miles of frozen country-

This painting by Howard Pyle (opposite) shows George Rogers Clark during the march from Kentucky to Kaskaskia. The French settlers along the Mississippi River helped Clark and his men in their campaign against the British.

The Illinois Regiment of the Virginia State Forces (above) fought the British in the Western territories during the Revolutionary War. Although many Indians sided with the British and attacked American settlements, some tribes were impressed by Clark's victories and were friendly to the Americans.

side, the Long Knives reached Vincennes. The British, taken by surprise, quickly surrendered; they had never expected attackers to appear out of the wilderness in the dead of winter. Clark's remarkable victory weakened Britain's control of the Illinois country and the rest of the frontier.

The Northwest Ordinance

In 1783, the Revolutionary War ended with Britain's defeat. The peace treaty that settled the conflict placed the Western border of the new United States of America at the Mississippi River. This land included a region known as "the Northwest Territory" —land between the Ohio River and the Great Lakes, including Illinois.

The new national government had to find the answers to difficult questions: How would the Northwest Territory be governed? Would slavery be allowed there? What relation would the new territory have to the original thirteen states?

This last question was especially difficult. Several of the original states claimed "outlets," or reserves, of land in the Northwest Territory. After Clark's capture of the Illinois country, for example, Virginia governor Patrick Henry had declared Illinois a county of that state.

The job of resolving these tough questions went to Thomas Jefferson, author of the Declaration of Independence. Jefferson drafted the Northwest Ordinance—one of the most far sighted documents in American history. Adopted by Congress in 1784, the ordinance went into effect, after some changes, in 1787.

Under its terms, the original states gave up their land claims in the Northwest Territory to the national

government. The region would be divided into territories. When the population of a territory reached 60,000, it could apply for admission to the Union as a state. Each new state would have the same rights as the original states. This was an important point. Without it, new territories would be little more than "colonies" of the older states to the east.

The ordinance called for between three and five states to be created from the Northwest Territory. It also outlawed slavery in the region. This provision would have an important impact on Illinois and the four other states—Indiana, Ohio, Michigan, and Wisconsin—that were later carved out of the Northwest Territory.

Thomas Jefferson (opposite, left), a future president of the United States, drafted the plan that would become the influential Northwest Ordinance. Jefferson's first version of the ordinance called for ten states to be created in the Northwest, with their names taken from Greek mythology.

This 1785 map (opposite, right) of the northwest parts of the United States shows the territory that would eventually become Illinois, Indiana, Michigan, Ohio, and Wisconsin.

The house depicted in this engraving (above) was built by French settlers at Kaskaskia in the American Bottom region of the Illinois country. The house is built of planks nailed to log posts, with a porch on all four sides.

Settlement and Statehood

The Northwest Ordinance had little to say about the rights of the people already living in the region—the Native Americans. When white settlers began moving into the land north of the Ohio River, they met fierce resistance. The fighting went on until 1794, when the U.S. Army won a major victory at the Battle of Fallen Timbers, fought in 1794 in what is now Ohio.

The following year, representatives from several Native American tribes signed the Treaty of Greenville. Among other provisions, the treaty called for Indians to give up several pieces of land in the Illinois country, including a thirty-six-square-mile plot on the southwestern shore of Lake Michigan. Emptying into the lake was a river the Native Americans called Checagou, or Eschicagau, which probably means "field of wild onions." In time this site would become Chicago, one of the nation's greatest cities.

It was already home to a small but busy trading post founded by Jean Baptiste Point du Sable. Not much is known about du Sable's early life, but he was probably born in Haiti, a descendant of African slaves. Around 1779, du Sable and his wife, a Native American of the Potawatomi tribe, built a house on what is now North Michigan Avenue in the heart of Chicago. For nearly two decades, du Sable prospered through trade with the local Native Americans.

In 1800—the year du Sable left Chicago—Congress organized the western part of the Northwest Territory, including Illinois, as the Indiana Territory. It took several years before the region attracted many new settlers. Still, by 1808, many people believed the time had come for Illinois to separate from the Indiana Territory. The following year, Congress organized the Territory of Illinois, with its capital at Kaskaskia. The northern boundary of the new territory ran all the way to Canada, so it included more than twice the land area of the present state. Maryland-born lawyer Ninian Edwards became the first territorial governor. His nephew, Nathaniel Pope, was the territorial delegate. (Under the Northwest Ordinance, each territory sent one nonvoting delegate to represent its interests in Congress.)

Most of the settlers who came to Illinois in the early 1800s made their homes in the southern part of the region. Settlement of northern Illinois was slowed because of a military disaster known as the Dearborn Massacre.

In 1803, the U.S. Army built Fort Dearborn near du Sable's old trading post. Over the next few years, a small community of traders and settlers grew up around the fort.

But war was brewing. Tensions between the United States and Britain

This lithograph (above) shows how Chicago looked at the beginning of the 19th century. The settlement included a small army post, a few houses belonging to traders, and several Native American villages.

English-born Morris Birkbeck (right) helped found a settlement on the southern Illinois prairie in 1817. His *Letters from Illinois*, published in 1818, convinced many people in England and other nations to move to the new state. Birkbeck was also active in the movement against slavery.

were high. Once again the British were arming Native Americans on the Northwest frontier, this time from forts in Canada. In June 1812, Britain and the United States went to war.

Fearing an Indian attack, the American commander in the Northwest, General William Hull, ordered Fort Dearborn's soldiers and the settlers living nearby to leave the fort and travel overland to Fort Wayne in present-day Indiana. On August 15, 1812, about 100 soldiers and civilians marched out of the fort. They had gone less than a mile when 400 Potawatomi warriors swept out of the forest with guns blazing.

The soldiers and settlers fought back fiercely, but within fifteen minutes half of them lay dead or dying.

The slaughter would have been even worse if a Potawatomi leader, Black Partridge, hadn't ordered his warriors to put down their weapons. The Potawatomis took the survivors prisoner and burned the fort. Until the army returned in 1816, Fort Dearborn's charred timbers were all that remained of the Chicago settlement.

This incident did not stop people from coming to Illinois, especially to the southern region. In the 1820s, Illinois began an era of swift settlement and development. In 1800, the non-Indian population of the Illinois country was only 2,500 people—about the same as during the French era. By 1818, more than 40,000 people had made Illinois their new home. In that year, territorial delegate Nathaniel Pope called on Congress to admit Illinois to the Union as a state. It was too early for such a move, because a population of 60,000 was required before a territory could become a state. But Pope was determined. With help from his nephew, Daniel Pope Cook, a young lawyer and newspaperman, Cook wrote many editorials in his paper, the *Western Intelligencer,* which gained public support for Illinois's statehood. On December 3, 1818, Pope's dream was realized, and Illinois became the twenty-first state, with Shadrach Bond as its first governor.

Illinois's first statehouse was a simple, two-story brick building rented for $4 a day. Twenty-nine representatives gathered on the first floor, while the fourteen senators met upstairs. The capital remained at Kaskaskia while a state constitution was drafted. In 1820, the capital moved to the new community of Vandalia. Seventeen years later Springfield became the state's permanent capital.

During the negotiations over statehood, Pope made a decision that would have great importance for Illinois. At first, Congress wanted the northern border of the state to run west from the southern tip of Lake Michigan to the Mississippi. Pope convinced Congress to move the border about forty miles north so that it included the site of Chicago. Without Pope's foresight, the greatest port and industrial city in the Midwest would be in Wisconsin.

Illinois settlers do chores outside their cabin in this lithograph (opposite). Children were expected to help out as soon as they were old enough. A young girl (far left) churns butter while her mother watches the baby.

Nephew and namesake of one of the earliest Americans to settle in Illinois, Shadrach Bond (below) served as both the first delegate to Congress from the Illinois Territory and the first governor of the state of Illinois.

New Arrivals, New Conflicts

What attracted newcomers to Illinois? More than anything else, it was the availability of cheap land. It took time, however, for land to become available to settlers. According to the Treaty of Greenville, most of Illinois belonged to the Indians. But in the early 1800s, most of the region's tribes signed treaties giving up their lands. The Native Americans sacrificed a great deal in these treaties, but there was little they could do in the face of white pressure.

After the government seized Indian land, it was surveyed into sections of several hundred acres and put up for sale at government land offices or at auctions. Pressure from settlers and politicians drove down both the price of land and the minimum amount a settler had to buy. By the 1820s, Illinois land sold at $1.25 per acre, and there was easy credit for buyers.

Even this price was too high for some people. Many Illinois settlers were "squatters"—pioneers who simply started a farm on a piece of land, hoping to buy it later. By 1828, two-thirds of the state's population were squatters, although most later gained legal title to their land. Along with the squatters came speculators—investors who bought up large pieces of land to sell to latecomers at a big profit.

Acquiring land was also an important concern for the Illinois Canal Commission, a group of officials who planned to build a canal from Lake Michigan west to the Illinois River. Such a waterway would help new settlers by bringing them supplies and giving them a way to send farm products back to the East. The commission raised money through Eastern investors and also with the help of the State Bank of Illinois. The opening of the canal helped encourage even more people to come to Illinois.

This lithograph (opposite) shows the Mississippi River town of Moline, Illinois. Descriptions of scenes like this—a country with ample waterways and clear, fertile land—increased the interest in Illinois settlement.

Between 1839 and 1842, the State Bank of Illinois printed "bank notes" (above, top) to help pay for the construction of roads, canals, and other "internal improvements" throughout the state, including the Illinois and Michigan Canal. Financial troubles in the late 1830s led to a total stop to the work on the canal in 1841, but it was finally completed in 1848. This engraving (above, bottom) shows one of the canal's fifteen locks.

Who were the Illinois pioneers? In the early years of statehood, most came from the Southern states. They arrived in Illinois by way of the Mississippi River, or later on "the National Road," which ran from Maryland to Vandalia. Most of the newcomers were poor farm families who arrived with little more than the clothes on their backs, a few tools, and perhaps a cow and a couple of horses.

After building a simple log cabin, the hard work of planting a crop of corn and vegetables began. The prairie soil was fertile, but so dense that it often broke wooden or iron plows. In the 1830s, an Illinois inventor, John Deere, solved this problem by developing a steel plow that easily cut prairie soil.

Many settlers were amazed at the richness of the land. "No weeds or grass sprang up on the ground the first year, and the corn needed no attention with plough or hoe," wrote a Greene County settler in 1820.

But life was often hard for pioneer families. Disease was common. Malaria, spread by mosquitoes, was so widespread that some called it "the Illinois shakes." Another illness, "Milk Sick," caused by drinking milk from cows who had eaten poisonous weeds, claimed the lives of many children.

After 1825, new groups of settlers began to arrive in Illinois. In that year, the Erie Canal opened for business. The canal linked the Atlantic Coast with the Great Lakes, opening up northern Illinois to settlement. The pioneers who came to this region were different from the Southerners who settled downstate Illinois. Many of the new arrivals were from New

England. Others were from Europe, especially Ireland and Germany. Thus, two waves of settlement—one from the South, one from the North and overseas—gave Illinois a regional "split" that is still felt today.

As white settlers moved into the Rock River region in northern Illinois, they clashed with one of the last Indian groups in the state—the Sauk and Fox tribe. In 1831, the federal government ordered the Sauk and Fox Indians to move to land across the Mississippi River, but a small group, followers of a leader named Black Hawk, returned to Illinois in 1832.

After several fights between Native Americans and settlers, the U.S. Army arrived. Together with volunteer soldiers, the soldiers chased Black Hawk and his 400 people out of Illinois and into what was then the Michigan Territory. In August, the last battle of the sad Black Hawk War was fought at Bad Axe on the Mississippi River in present-day Wisconsin. The Sauk and Fox Indians tried to cross to the western bank of the river under heavy fire from the soldiers. An unknown number of Native Americans died, including many women and children. Taken prisoner, Black Hawk died on an Iowa reservation in 1838. Settlement continued at a fast pace in the 1830s and 1840s. By the early 1850s, Illinois had a population of more than 1 million, making it the fourth-largest state.

Once in Illinois, a pioneer family would choose a site for its homestead—usually a level piece of land with a spring or stream nearby—and build a log cabin. Ideal dwellings for frontier life, log cabins could be built quickly and required few tools and nails (opposite, left). Settlers worked hard—farming, hunting, sewing, cooking, and cleaning. Washing (opposite, right) had to be done in a nearby stream as there were no wells or running water.

The Sauk and Fox leader, Black Hawk (above), wanted only to plant corn when he led his followers into the Rock Island area in the spring of 1832. The war that followed marked the end of 150 years of conflicts between Indians and whites in Illinois.

Nation and State Divided

Illinois would soon be the scene of much struggle and debate over slavery, an issue that divided Americans and led them to civil war in 1861. Most people in downstate Illinois had roots in the South, so they weren't troubled by slavery. There was strong antislavery feeling, however, among settlers who came from the East, and the European immigrants who chose northern and central Illinois as their home. Many of these people weren't opposed to slavery in the Southern states, but they didn't want it to spread into the new territories west of the Mississippi.

Others went further. These people were called abolitionists, because they believed in abolishing, or outlawing, slavery throughout the nation. The clash between proslavery and antislavery Illinoisans sometimes turned violent. In 1837, a proslavery mob destroyed an abolitionist newspaper office in Alton and killed the paper's editor, Elijah Lovejoy.

The 1858 U.S. Senate election showed how deeply Illinois, and the nation, were divided. The candidates were Abraham Lincoln, a member of the new Republican Party, and the incumbent, Stephen Douglas, a Democrat and the most powerful politician in the state. Douglas—a short, plump man nicknamed "the little giant"— believed that people in the Western

territories should decide for themselves whether or not to permit slavery. Tall, lean Lincoln was not an abolitionist, but he felt that slavery shouldn't be allowed to spread.

In the summer of 1858, the two men met at seven different sites in face-to-face debates. The campaign drew national attention as both men argued their cases before huge crowds. Lincoln won praise for his well-reasoned speeches, but he narrowly lost the senate election to Douglas.

Despite his defeat in the senate election, the debates made Abraham Lincoln a national figure. When the Republican Party met to pick a candidate for the election of 1860, Lincoln was a contender for the nomination.

Thanks to the influence of Joseph Medill, an editor of the *Chicago*

Driven out of Missouri in 1833, newspaper publisher Elijah Lovejoy moved to Alton, Illinois. When he published an editorial in 1837 calling slavery "an awful evil and sin," a proslavery mob attacked his warehouse (opposite). Lovejoy was shot and killed in the attack.

Born in Kentucky and raised on the Indiana frontier, Abraham Lincoln moved to Illinois at the age of twenty-one. As a young man living in the town of New Salem, he worked splitting rails for fences, as shown in this painting (top).

Lincoln (at podium) speaks before a crowd during the famous Lincoln-Douglas debates of 1858 (right). Douglas stands behind him. The debates caught the attention of the nation: "The battle of the Union," said a Washington, D.C., newspaper, "is to be fought in Illinois."

Tribune newspaper, Chicago was chosen to host the Republican Convention. More than 30,000 delegates and tourists crowded into the city for the event. The delegates met in a huge, hastily built wooden hall known as "the Wigwam." On May 17, Lincoln won the party's nomination.

Lincoln went on to win the presidency in a four-way race. (One of his opponents was Stephen Douglas, candidate of the Northern wing of the Democrat party.) After Lincoln's victory, Southern states began to secede, or withdraw in protest, from the Union to form the Confederate States of America. In April 1861, the Civil War began when Confederate forces attacked a Union fort in the harbor at Charleston, South Carolina. Although many Illinoisans sympathized with the Confederacy, the state remained loyal to the Union. Pro-Confederate "Copperheads" in Illinois's downstate counties protested the war, but they never really threatened the Union war effort.

In fact, Illinois did much to help the Union win the war. About 260,000 Illinois men served in the Union army and navy, and 35,000 of them lost their lives. Grain and beef from Illinois fed Union forces. The downstate city of Cairo was a major base for the Union armies in the South.

Many Illinois civilians worked to improve living conditions and medical care for Illinois soldiers in the field. The most famous of these volunteers was a Galesburg woman, Mary Ann Bickerdyke. "Mother" Bickerdyke ran field hospitals and laundries, transported medical supplies, and organized a nursing service to care for sick and wounded soldiers. She was reportedly the only woman that hardbitten General William Tecumseh Sherman allowed to travel on the road with his army.

Illinois's greatest contribution was the leadership of Abraham Lincoln. Through four long years of war, Lincoln held the Union together and finally led it to victory. The war was almost over when an assassin's bullet ended Lincoln's life in April 1865.

A few weeks later, the train carrying Lincoln's body home for burial arrived in Springfield. Tearful mourners from all over the state walked silently past the coffin of Illinois's most famous resident, and one of the nation's greatest presidents.

This lithograph (opposite) shows Union general Ulysses S. Grant (lower right, with telescope) during the siege of Vicksburg, Mississippi, in 1863. Born in Ohio, Grant was a resident of Galena, Illinois, when the war broke out.

This photograph (below) shows Abraham Lincoln's house in Springfield draped in black mourning cloth following the president's assassination in April 1865. Lincoln is buried in Springfield's Oak Ridge cemetery.

PART TWO

CHANGES AND CHALLENGES

Illinois's natural past and high-tech future meet at the Fermi National Accelerator Laboratory, or Fermilab, in Batavia. A herd of buffalo, part of the lab's environmental conservation program, can be seen in the foreground.

Chicago became one of the nation's leading cities in the decades after the Civil War, despite its near destruction by fire in 1871. The city's rise to become the transportation and manufacturing capital of the Midwest was marked by struggles between business and labor. The state faced many challenges in the 20th century, from the gang wars of Chicago in the 1920s to the Depression of the 1930s and the start of industrial decline in the 1970s. Today, with a diverse population and economy, Illinois remains at the crossroads of American life.

The Rise of Chicago

Throughout the French, British, and early American eras, southern Illinois was home to most of the region's people and trade. That began to change by the middle of the 19th century, and even more so after the Civil War. Northern Illinois and its chief city, Chicago, rose in importance—not only to the state and the Midwest, but to the entire country.

Location and transportation were the key to Chicago's success. Chicago lies at the natural meeting-point of North America. The Great Lakes give Chicago access to the East Coast, while nearby rivers connect with the Mississippi, gateway to the West and the South. Canals and railroads improved on nature, making Chicago the nation's transportation hub.

In the years after the War of 1812, however, Chicago was home to only a few soldiers and traders. More people arrived after the opening of the Erie Canal in 1825. Still, there were only

Barges loaded with grain leave Chicago in this engraving. In the decade after the Civil War, more than 65 million bushels of Midwestern wheat and corn passed through the port of Chicago each year.

150 houses in the area in 1833, when an English visitor called Chicago "an upstart village." By 1837, however, the population rose to 4,000, and Chicago officially became a city.

Money problems held up Chicago's progress. A nationwide economic depression began in 1837. Banks and businesses failed throughout the state. But Illinois recovered quickly, and in the 1840s Chicago started to boom as immigrants going west and farm products going east crossed paths in the busy city.

In 1848, the Illinois and Michigan Canal opened, giving Chicago an improved water link to the West. In the same year, the first railroad line reached the city. In 1856, the Illinois Central Railroad arrived, cutting travel time between Springfield and Chicago from three days to twelve hours. Engineers deepened the sandy mouth of the Chicago River, making it easier for ships to load and unload cargo.

The Union armies needed huge amounts of grain, horses, and meat during the four years of the Civil War, and much of these supplies came by way of Chicago. During the war years, as many as 100 trains a day rolled through the city.

By the end of the Civil War, Chicago was booming. "The gem of the prairie," as some called the growing city, was fast becoming the commercial capital of the Midwest.

Among the leading merchants of the city was Marshall Field, who had arrived in Chicago from Massachusetts in 1856. In 1865, Field and two partners built "the marble palace," a six-story department store on State Street. Field, Palmer & Leiter (later known as Marshall Field) changed the way Chicagoans—and eventually all Americans—did their shopping. The store was one of the first establishments to sell a variety of goods under one roof, and Field introduced such business innovations as standardized pricing and allowing customers to return unsatisfactory merchandise.

By 1870, Chicago's population passed the 300,000 mark. To house so many newcomers, Chicago turned to a new kind of building—the balloon-frame house. Invented by Vermont-born Chicagoan George Washington Snow, the balloon-frame

Dwight Lyman Moody came to Chicago as a salesman in 1853. Turning to preaching, he opened a mission in the city and went on to become one of the greatest religious figures of the late 19th century. This photograph (opposite, top) shows Moody (in top hat) with orphans at one of his Chicago missions. The boys had fanciful street names such as "Jacky Candle," "Sniderick," "Rag-breeches Cadet," and "Madden the Butcher."

This early carpentry handbook (right) showed that even amateur carpenters could build a house using balloon-frame construction, which became the standard in Chicago during the mid-19th century.

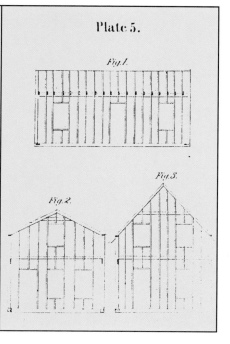

PLATE 5.

Plate 5 is designed to represent a balloon frame of a building a story and a half high, 16 by 28 feet on the ground, with 12 feet studding. Two end elevations are given, in order to exhibit different styles of roofs. Fig. 2 being a plain roof, of a quarter pitch; and Fig. 3 a Gothic roof, the rafters rising 14 inches to the foot.

Framing the Sills.

Solid timber, 8 inches square, being furnished for the sills of this building, the first business is to frame these. The carpenter will seldom have timber furnished to his hand which is perfectly square throughout its length; by carelessness in hewing, or by the process of seasoning after being hewed, it will most commonly have become irregular and winding.

Work Sides.

Having first selected the two best adjoining sides, one for the upper side and the other for the front, called *work sides*, they should *be taken out of wind* in the following manner.

To take Timber out of Wind.

Place off a spot on one of the work sides, a few inches from one end, and draw a pencil line square across it; then place the blade of a square upon this line, allowing the tongue to hang down as a plummet, to keep the blade on its edge. Leave the square in this position, and go to the other end of the sill, and place another square upon it, in the same manner; then sight across the two squares, and see if they are level or parallel with each other. If not, make them so, by cutting off the spots under the squares till they become so; then make the other work side square with this one, at these two spots, and draw a pencil mark square across both sides; these marks are called *plumb spots*.

On the upper side of the timber, strike a chalk-line, from one end to the other, at two inches from the front edge; this will be the front line for mortices for studs. On this line measure the length of the

(50)

33

house was made of light planks fastened to a frame with iron nails. People called Snow's invention the balloon house because some thought the new-style house would blow away like a balloon in a stiff wind. It didn't. Balloon-frame houses were cheap and simple, and they took much less time to build than brick, stone, or heavy timber houses. They were ideal for a fast-growing city like Chicago. Unfortunately, a city full of such houses was in danger when fire broke out. And on the night of October 8, 1871, Chicago went up in flames.

According to a popular story, the fire began when a cow knocked over a kerosene lantern in a barn behind a Mrs. O'Leary's house on DeKoven Street. The story isn't true, but a fire did start on the O'Leary property around 9:00 PM. Dry weather, wooden buildings, and a strong wind helped spread the blaze. The flames soon jumped the Chicago River, and a wall of fire moved across the city. "A column of flames would shoot up from a burning building, catch the force of the wind, and strike the next one," wrote a survivor.

When the fire burned out around midnight on October 9, about 300 people were dead and 90,000 homeless. An area of more than three square miles—the heart of the city— was a smoking ruin.

Chicagoans flee across the Randolph Street Bridge during the devastating fire of October 8–9, 1871. The disaster caused $200 million in property damage and destroyed almost 20,000 buildings.

Immigration and Labor

Chicago started to rebuild almost immediately. Some stores and businesses reopened in shacks on burned-out lots just days after the fire ended. Bankers in New York and other cities loaned money so new construction could begin. To make sure the disaster would never happen again, the city government passed strict building codes requiring fireproof materials to be used in new buildings.

By 1873, Chicago was not only back on its feet, but growing again. In 1880, the city's population stood at about 500,000—150,000 more people than at the time of the fire.

In the years after the fire, Chicago grew into a great industrial city. Chicago became the place where cattle from Texas were slaughtered, where wheat from Kansas was stored in great grain elevators, where iron ore from Minnesota was turned into steel, and where businesspeople made and lost huge fortunes. By the turn of the 20th century, Chicago was the financial and commercial capital of the Midwest and the second largest city in the United States.

All this was accomplished by the hard work of hundreds of thousands of immigrants from Ireland, Germany, Poland, and a dozen other nations. In the 1880s, at least half of Chicago's population was foreign born. These people worked ten- or twelve-hour

days for low pay in the city's factories, mills, slaughterhouses, and meat-packing plants. Working conditions were often unsafe and unhealthy.

At this time, governments were mostly unwilling to pass laws to protect workers, so workers took matters into their own hands. They tried to form labor unions, hoping to win better treatment from business owners by joining together. Many businesspeople, however, saw the unions as a threat to their profits. The last decades of the 19th century saw many conflicts between business and labor, some of these clashes became violent, such as the Chicago railroad strike and the Haymarket riot.

The ashes had barely cooled before Chicago-ans began to rebuild their city (opposite). Much of the heavy work of the reconstruction of the city fell to immigrant laborers.

Tensions between business and labor grew during the 19th century. Strikes often became violent. An illustration from *Harper's Weekly* newspaper (above) shows an explosion in Haymarket Square during a labor rally.

In the summer of 1877, for example, Chicago became caught up in a national railroad strike. The strike began when the Baltimore & Ohio Railroad announced a pay cut for its employees. Within days, railroad workers in Ohio, Pennsylvania and Illinois stopped work and blocked trains in a show of support for the

Baltimore & Ohio strikers. On July 26, 20,000 Chicago workers demonstrated in favor of the strike. Policemen met the demonstrators with force, aided by "volunteers" hired by the city's business community; thirty-five people were killed.

More lives were lost in the Haymarket Riot, which took place in Chicago in 1886. Six workers had been killed during a strike at the McCormick farm equipment plant on May 3. Labor leaders called for a protest rally to be held in Haymarket Square the next night.

The rally began peacefully. Suddenly a bomb exploded. Shots rang out as police and demonstrators fired at each other. When the smoke cleared, seven people—five policemen and two civilians—lay dead. No one was sure who threw the bomb or killed the policemen, but eight labor leaders were soon arrested. A jury found them guilty of starting a riot. All but one was sentenced to death, although three later had their sentences reduced to life in prison. Four of the convicted men were hanged. Another killed himself in jail.

In the years after the riot, however, some people became convinced the labor leaders had done nothing wrong and that their trial had been unfair. Among them was Illinois's German-born governor, John Peter Altgeld. In 1893, Altgeld ordered the three surviving prisoners freed. It was a courageous move, because many important people still believed the labor leaders were guilty of serious crimes.

The following year, another labor dispute shook the Chicago area. When workers at the Pullman railroad car factory went out on strike, railroad workers around the country also stopped work to support them. The strikes halted trains carrying the U.S. Mail, so President Grover Cleveland ordered the strikers back to work. Governor Altgeld again became a figure of controversy when he protested the president's use of federal troops to move mail trains through Chicago.

Over the years, the union movement did succeed in winning better pay, hours, and conditions for many workers, but life remained hard for the immigrant families crowded into Chicago's slums. At that time, the government didn't provide social services to help poor people.

Jane Addams, a social reformer, was shocked by living conditions in the city's immigrant neighborhoods and decided to do something to improve them. In 1889, Addams and her friend Ellen Starr moved into a rundown building on Halsted Street. They named it Hull-House. Addams, Starr, and other volunteers taught English, cared for the children of working women, and provided medical care and medicine to poor people. Soon, the "settlement house movement" that began in Chicago spread to other American cities.

A scene from the Pullman Strike of 1894 (above): Angry strikers wave fists and clubs as federal troops guard a train steaming out of Chicago's stockyards. The two-month strike tied up trains all over the country.

George Pullman (right) designed the first railroad sleeping cars in 1858 and later established a "company town" outside Chicago to build them. The 1894 strike began when Pullman cut his workers' pay by one-third, even though the nation was in the middle of an economic depression.

Illinois Enters the 20th Century

By 1900, the population of Illinois had reached 4,821,000, making it the third-largest state. About 28 percent of Illinois's people lived in Chicago, which had grown to cover an area of almost 200 square miles as the new century began. One out of every four Illinoisans was foreign-born; in Chicago, the figure was three out of every four.

Much of Illinois, however, remained rural. The homesteads of the early 1800s were now neat, productive farms. But times were often difficult for the state's farmers. After the Civil War, falling prices for farm products forced many rural people out of business. Some downstate counties lost population as farmers gave up in Illinois and moved away.

Farmers were especially angry at the railroads that brought their goods to market, and the owners of the elevators and mills where corn and wheat were stored and processed. The farmers believed the owners of these businesses kept their rates unfairly high to make the biggest possible profits.

Just as factory workers organized unions, farmers in Illinois and other states joined together to win better treatment. They succeeded: In the last decades of the 19th century, the state legislature passed laws to ensure fairer railroad rates.

At the beginning of the 20th century, Chicago was a vibrant and impressive city. This photograph (left) shows one of the city's architectural masterpieces, the Carson Pirie Scott Department Store, designed by Louis Sullivan and completed in 1904.

Outside of the city, farmers struggled to meet the rising rates of the railroads, mills, and grain elevators that processed their wheat and corn. Farmers would deliver their harvest to local grain elevators (above) where the grain would be weighed and stored before it was loaded onto railroad cars and sent to Chicago. From Chicago the grain would be shipped throughout the country.

In the 20th century, the Progressive movement in Illinois politics led to the passage of other far-reaching laws. The Progessives believed that American society could be improved by adopting reforms geared mainly toward the poor and working class. Illinois was one of the first states to outlaw child labor and to require employers to pay damages to workers injured on the job. Illinois made history in 1913 when it became the first state east of the Mississippi to allow women to vote in presidential elections, seven years before a constitutional amendment guaranteed the vote to all American women.

Illinois also made great contributions to American architecture and literature. The first true skyscraper—a tall building built around a steel frame—was Chicago's ten story Home Insurance Company Building. The work of architect William LeBaron Jenney, the building was completed in 1885. Other architects, especially Louis Sullivan and Daniel Burnham, followed Jenney in developing this uniquely American form of architecture.

In literature, Illinois novelists like Frank Norris, Upton Sinclair, and Theodore Dreiser won national fame. Illinois poets included Edgar Lee Masters and Vachel Lindsay. Their works were often published in *Poetry: A Magazine of Verse*, an important literary magazine founded by Chicagoan Harriet Monroe.

The most famous Illinois poet of this era was Galesburg-born Carl Sandburg. In his 1914 poem *Chicago*, Sandburg gave a famous description of the city:

Hog Butcher for the World,
Tool Maker, Stacker of Wheat,
Player with Railroads and the
Nation's Freight Handler,
Stormy, Husky, Brawling,
City of the Broad Shoulders.

African Americans first arrived in the state in large numbers in the early 1900s. Around the time the United States entered World War I, thousands of African Americans began moving from the South to Chicago and other cities, attracted by jobs in wartime industries. Many white Illinoisans were angered by the wave of black immigration—partly out of prejudice, and also from fear that the newcomers would take jobs away from whites.

These tensions resulted in some of the worst racial violence in American history. In 1917, a white mob burned African-American homes in East St. Louis; at least forty-eight people were killed in the fighting. Two years later, violence spread to Chicago. When whites killed a young black man at a "whites only" city beach in July 1919, police refused to make any arrests. A full week of riots followed in which fifteen whites and twenty-four African Americans died. Other victims suffered injuries and property damage.

Chicago was a center for architectural innovation at the turn of the century. Louis Henri Sullivan (right) was one of the fathers of the modern skyscraper—challenging America to live and work in buildings over ten stories tall. He influenced a generation of architects and designers with his belief that "form follows function."

Illinois militia (National Guard) troops patrol Chicago's South Side (below) after the bloody rioting of July 1919. The East St. Louis and Chicago riots were the worst incidents of racial violence in America since the Civil War.

From Prohibition to World War II

Despite the hostility of many whites, African Americans continued to come to Chicago in the 1920s. Most of them settled on the city's South Side. By 1930, African Americans made up 7 percent of the city's population, up from 4 percent in 1918. The voice of the city's growing black community was the Chicago *Defender* newspaper, which was read by African Americans all over the country. And in 1928, voters from the South Side sent Oscar DePriest, a Republican, to Washington as the first black congressman since the 1870s.

The 1920s were mostly prosperous years for America. But in Illinois, this prosperity was marred by the violence and corruption surrounding Prohibition, which became law in 1919. Prohibition began with the passage of the Eighteenth Amendment which outlawed the manufacture, sale, or transportation of alcohol. Prohibition was an attempt to end the many problems caused by alcohol abuse. Unfortunately, the law backfired. Many Americans wanted to continue drinking alcohol, law or no law. Criminals saw that they could make a lot of money by bootlegging, providing illegal alcohol to speakeasies (secret drinking clubs).

The problem was especially bad in Chicago, where well-organized criminal gangs were already operating. The gangsters wasted no time in moving into the bootlegging business. Politicians, judges, and police were paid off to look the other way as truckloads of beer and whiskey arrived at the speakeasies. Gangsters used assault, murder, and other terror tactics to drive rival gangs out of business. Innocent people sometimes got caught in the crossfire.

The most powerful Chicago gangster was Alphonse Capone. By the late 1920s, the Capone gang controlled most of the liquor trade in the city and its suburbs. The worst incident of Al Capone's reign was the St. Valentine's Day Massacre in February 1929, when Capone's men machine-

gunned to death seven members of a competing gang in a garage on the city's North Side.

Popular movies about Chicago gangsters made in the 1930s and 1940s, have given many people a mistaken impression of the city. The lawlessness of Chicago in the 1920s was not worse than in other cities.

Congress finally ended Prohibition in 1933. By that time, Illinoisans, and all Americans, had other things to worry about. A stock market crash in 1929 led to the Great Depression, a nationwide economic slump that hit Illinois especially hard. In the early 1930s, 1.5 million Illinois citizens were out of work.

Master mobster Al Capone, shown here in 1930 (opposite), finally went to prison in 1932 for failing to pay his taxes, not for bootlegging or murder.

The Depression hit farmers and city dwellers alike in Illinois. Local governments set up relief efforts (above) to distribute food and supplies to those in need.

The federal government tried to help matters with programs like the CCC (Civil Conservation Corps), which hired unemployed people to build roads, parks, and other public works. The CCC was especially active in downstate Illinois. In Chicago and other industrial areas, the state and federal governments spent millions of

Nobel Prize-winner Enrico Fermi led the scientists who produced the first controlled atomic chain reaction in 1942. Fermi, a refugee from Italy who became a U.S. citizen in 1944, served as a professor at the University of Chicago from 1945 until his death in 1954.

dollars to provide relief for the many jobless, hungry citizens. At one point, the federal government was spending more money on Illinois than on New York and Pennsylvania (the largest two states at that time) combined.

Despite these measures, the Depression continued throughout the 1930s. With the coming of World War II, however, economic bad times turned to boom times almost overnight.

The state's farms, factories, and mines all worked mightily for the war effort. The Rock Island Arsenal in northern Illinois made most of the artillery shells for the U.S. military, while thousands of tanks rolled off the assembly lines at the Caterpillar tractor plant in Peoria. Illinois farms helped feed the nation and exported food to a war-ravaged world. Nearly one million Illinois men and women served in the military—one out of every eight Illinoisans—and 22,000 gave their lives.

One of the most important events of the war took place not on a battlefield, but in a laboratory at the University of Chicago. On December 2, 1942, a team of scientists led by Enrico Fermi succeeded in creating the world's first controlled nuclear chain reaction. The experiment proved that an atomic bomb could be made. Thirty-two months later, American warplanes dropped atomic bombs on two Japanese cities, officially ending World War II.

Decades of Growth and Change

The decades after World War II were a time of change for Illinois. The state continued to grow, but other areas of the country grew faster. Illinois went from being the third-largest state (in total population) in 1950 to the sixth-largest just thirty years later. More and more people moved from farms to cities, until nine-tenths of the state's population lived in urban areas.

The regional split between Chicago and the rest of Illinois grew wider. By the 1980s, more than half of the residents in the state lived in the Chicago metropolitan area, which came to include parts of both Wisconsin and Indiana. Starting in 1950, however, the city itself began to lose population as many people moved to the fast-growing suburban communities of Cook County.

Chicago remained one of the nation's great transportation hubs, even in the jet age. In 1946, O'Hare Airport opened outside the city. The

Chicago's lakefront skyline became especially impressive in the decades after World War II. The tower in the John Hancock Center dominates this photograph—when it was completed in 1969 it was the tallest skyscraper in the Midwest.

facility became the busiest airport in the world, boasting more than 2,000 takeoffs and landings a day by the early 1990s.

Water transportation, always important to Chicago, got a boost with the opening of the St. Lawrence Seaway in 1959. The Seaway, built together by the United States and Canada, connected the Great Lakes with the Atlantic Ocean. Before the Seaway opened, only small ships from the lakes could reach the Atlantic, because the St. Lawrence River was too shallow. One of the great engineering feats of all time, the Seaway project deepened the river and improved the locks (connecting waterways) that allowed ships to go from the lakes to the river and finally out to sea. When the St. Lawrence Seaway was completed, Chicago became an international port; ships from all over the world could now travel to and from the city.

During the 1950s, two Illinois politicians attracted national attention. The first was Adlai Stevenson, a member of a family that had long been active in state and local politics. The second was Richard J. Daley, a union organizer's son who began the first of twenty-one years as mayor of Chicago in 1955.

In 1948, Stevenson, a Democrat, was elected governor. He was the party's presidential candidate in 1952 and 1956, but was defeated both times by Republican Dwight Eisenhower.

The intelligent, well-spoken Stevenson served only one term, but he helped improve Illinois's political reputation. The state was always known for its free-and-easy politics, where votes were sometimes bought and sold, and politicians sometimes took orders from powerful party organizations instead of from voters.

Daley governed the city and controlled the Cook County machine at the same time. His opponents believed he held too much power. His supporters, however, liked to say that Daley made Chicago "a city that worked." The mayor kept the city services running, and Chicago's economy stayed strong while other cities went into decline.

The completion of the St. Lawrence Seaway connected Chicago's ports to the Atlantic Ocean. In this photograph (opposite), grain is loaded onto ocean tankers to be shipped around the world.

Police in riot gear (above) form a barricade against demonstrators who protested during the trial of the Chicago Seven. This group of radicals was arrested for plotting to incite a riot during the 1968 Democratic National Convention.

Daley's reputation, and Chicago's, suffered a blow in 1968, when the city hosted the Democratic Presidential Convention. This was at the height of the Vietnam War, and many young people gathered in Chicago to protest the conflict. Daley ordered the police to break up antiwar demonstrations.

Jane Byrne, shown here speaking to supporters at Chicago's O'Hare Airport, defeated Michael Bilandic to become the city's first woman mayor in 1979. Before her election as mayor, Byrne served in the Daley administration as consumer sales commissioner.

They did so with violence that was shown on the television news.

Mayor Daley became such a part of city life that people pronounced his name as one word—Maredaley. But Daley's influence went beyond Illinois. Because Daley was such a powerful Democrat, his support was sought by those seeking the presidential nomination. The mayor did much to help John F. Kennedy's presidential campaign in 1960.

Daley died in office in 1976. Three years later, Jane Byrne became the city's first woman mayor. By the time Byrne left office in 1983, however, Chicago was no longer America's "second city"—Los Angeles had pulled ahead in population, putting Chicago third behind New York and Los Angeles.

Illinois—Today and Tomorrow

Middle-class people moved out of Chicago and into the growing suburbs, where life seemed safer and cleaner. As a result, city services declined, and overcrowding and unemployment rose in the city's poorer neighborhoods. The 1980s also saw a sharp increase in Chicago's crime rate.

New leaders worked hard to solve the city's problems. Among them was Harold Washington, who became the city's first African-American mayor in 1983. Washington served until his death in 1987, but his term was marked by political battles with the city council.

Washington was succeeded by another African-American mayor, Eugene Sawyer. In 1989, Richard M. Daley, son of Richard J. Daley, took office as mayor after defeating Sawyer in a special election. He was reelected in 1991.

Other Illinois politicians have achieved national importance in recent years. Republican Lynn Martin, a former Illinois representative, served as secretary of labor from 1991 to 1993. Senator Paul Simon was a contender for the Democratic presidential nomination in 1988 and 1992; in the House, Democratic representative Dan Rostenkowski served as chairman of the powerful Ways and Means Committee. And in 1992,

Illinois voters made history by sending Democrat Carol Moseley-Braun to Washington as the nation's first African-American woman senator.

Economically, the 1980s and early 1990s were difficult times for many Illinoisans. For the state's farmers, the 1980s seemed like a repeat of the

Harold Washington, Chicago's first African-American mayor, is shown speaking in front of a portrait of longtime mayor Richard J. Daley. Before becoming mayor in 1983, Washington served in the Illinois House of Representatives and Senate, as well as the U.S. Congress.

Mayor Richard J. Daley
1902–1976

1870s. In the 1970s and early 1980s, crop prices and land values were high, so many farmers in Illinois and other Midwestern states took out loans and mortgages to buy farm equipment and expand their land.

After about 1981, however, crop prices began to fall, and over the next few years, the value of Illinois farmland dropped by as much as 33 percent in some counties. Many farmers found it impossible to keep up loan and mortgage payments. More and more farmers in Illinois were forced to auction off their farm machinery and sell their land to pay their debts. To raise money to help farmers keep their land, a group of rock and country music stars held a "Farm Aid" benefit concert in Champaign, Illinois, in 1985. The concert drew national attention to the farm crisis, but it wasn't until after 1988 that conditions started to improve for farmers in Illinois and other states.

Industrial Illinois was hard hit in the 1980s, too. Competition from overseas, a decline in the economic importance of manufacturing, and a shift in population from "Rust Belt" states like Illinois to the "Sun Belt" states of the South and West—all combined to force many Illinois factories to shut down. By the end of the decade, the unemployment rate hit 50 percent in some Illinois communities.

Illinois benefited from the computer and telecommunications boom of the 1980s and 1990s. High-tech companies moved to the state, attracted by Illinois's skilled workforce and many major universities and research centers.

In the summer of 1993, the Mississippi flooded, ravaging riverside communities throughout the state. The nation saw Illinoisans from all walks of life on the television news working together to repair flood damage and keep the waters from spreading. The aftermath of the 1993 floods made one thing clear to all Americans. The pioneer spirit—the spirit of the people who settled the prairies, rebuilt Chicago after the devastating fire, and made their state great—is still alive and well in the Illinois of the 1990s.

Eighty thousand music fans came out in the rain to support the nation's farmers by attending the Farm Aid concert (opposite). The fundraiser, organized by country music singer Willie Nelson, took place at the University of Illinois Memorial Stadium in Champaign.

These satellite photos (below) of the area around Quincy, Illinois, show the damage caused by the Mississippi River's flooding in the summer of 1993. The photograph at left shows the river under normal conditions; the dark area on the photograph at right shows the spread of the floodwaters.

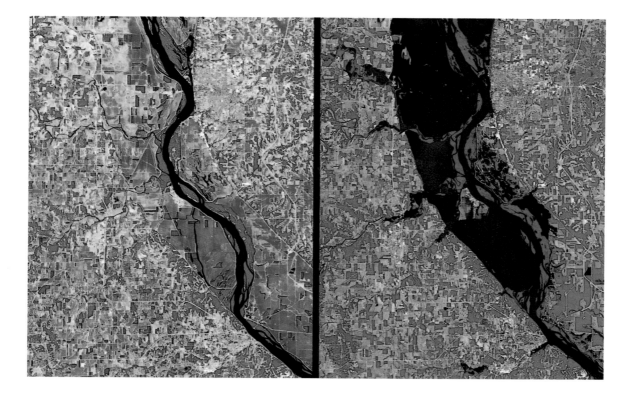

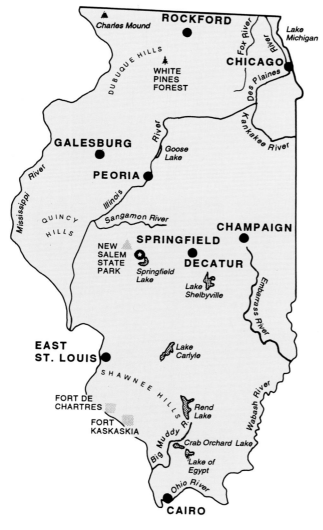

Land area:
56,345 square miles, of which 700 are inland water. Ranks 24th in size.

Major rivers:
The Big Muddy; the Des Plaines; the Fox; the Illinois; the Mississippi; the Ohio; the Sangamon; the Wabash.

Highest point: Charles Mound in Jo Daviess County, 1,235 ft.

Major bodies of water:
Crab Orchard Lake; Goose Lake; Lake Carlyle; Lake of Egypt; Lake Shelbyville; Springfield Lake. The state also has 65 miles of coastline on Lake Michigan.

Climate:
Average January temperature: 21°F
Average July temperature: 73°F

Population: 11,631,131 (1992)
Rank: 6th
  1900: 4,821,550
  1820: 55,211

Population of major cities (1992):

Chicago	2,783,726
Rockford	139,943
Peoria	113,504
Springfield	105,227
Decatur	83,885
East St. Louis	40,944

Ethnic breakdown by percentage (1990):

White	74.8%
African American	14.6%
Hispanic	7.9%
Asian	2.4%
Native American	0.2%
Other	0.1%

Economy:
  Manufacturing; agriculture (corn, wheat, soybeans, oats, and livestock); printing and publishing; finance.

State government:
  Legislature: The General Assembly consists of a 59-member senate and an 118-member house of representatives. Senators can be elected to either 2- or 4-year terms; representatives serve 2-year terms.
  Governor: The governor is elected to a 4-year term.
  Courts: The state's judicial system has 3 levels of courts—supreme, appellate, and circuit.
State capital: Springfield

State Flag

First adopted in 1915, the state flag features the state seal on a white background. In 1969, the flag design was changed to include the name "Illinois" below the seal.

State Seal

The state seal was adopted in 1868. It features an eagle grasping a scroll with the state motto, the sun rising on the prairie, and a shield representing the original colonies.

State Motto

"State Sovereignty, National Union."

State Nickname

To honor its most famous citizen, the General Assembly chose "Land of Lincoln" as the state's official slogan in 1955. Illinois is also known as "the Prairie State."

Places

Adler Planetarium, Chicago

Apple River Canyon State Park, Warren

Art Institute of Chicago, Chicago

Brookfield Zoo Brookfield

Burpee Museum of Natural History, Rockford

Cahokia Mounds, Collinsville

Carl Sandburg's Birthplace, Galesburg

Chain O'Lakes State Park, McHenry

Chicago Historical Society, Chicago

Chicago Portage National Historic Site, Chicago

Dickson Mounds State Memorial, Havana

Du Sable Museum of African American History, Chicago

Early American Museum, Mahomet

Elijah Lovejoy Monument, Alton

Field Museum of Natural History, Chicago

Fort de Chartres State Park, Prairie du Rocher

Fort Kaskaskia State Park, Chester

Giant City State Park, Makanda

Hauberg Indian Museum, Rock Island

Hull-House, Chicago

Illinois State Museum, Springfield

John Deere Historic Site, Grand Detour

to See

John G. Shedd Aquarium, Chicago

Joseph Smith Home, Nauvoo

Kankakee River State Park, Kankakee

Lincoln Home National Historic Site, Springfield

Lincoln Park Zoo, Chicago

Lincoln's Trail State Memorial, Lawrenceville

Metamora Court House State Memorial, Metamora

Mississippi Palisades State Park, Savanna

Morton Arboretum, Lisle

Museum of Science and Industry, Chicago

New Salem State Park, Petersburg

Old Market House State Memorial, Galena

Old State Capitol, Springfield

Oriental Institute Museum, Chicago

Pere Marquette State Park, Grafton

Pierre Menard Memorial, Chester

Robie House, Chicago

Shawneetown State Memorial, Shawneetown

Starved Rock State Park, Utica

Stephen A. Douglas Tomb, Chicago

Vandalia State House, Vandalia

White Pines Forest State Park, Oregon

Ulysses S. Grant Home, Galena

State Flower

In 1907, Illinois schoolchildren took part in a vote to choose an official state flower. The winner was the native violet, a small purplish flower found throughout the state.

State Bird

Another vote by schoolchildren in 1929 named the cardinal Illinois's official state bird. About eight inches long, the cardinal is known for its bright red plumage and whistle-like song.

State Tree

The white oak was chosen as the state tree in 1907. Also known as the stave oak, it is a large tree with gray bark.

Illinois History

c. 300 BC First traces of Indian culture

c. 1500 Illiniweks dominate the region

1673 Jacques Marquette and Louis Jolliet explore Illinois

1680 La Salle builds a fort near the site of Peoria

1692–1703 The French build settlements in Cahokia and Kaskaskia

1765 British win control of Illinois region from France

1770s Jean Baptiste du Sable founds a trading post on the site of the future Chicago

1778 George Rogers Clark takes Kaskaskia from British in Revolutionary War

1787 Northwest Ordinance sets up government for Illinois region

1794 Illinois Indians defeated at Battle of Fallen Timbers; Illinois opens for settlement

1809 Congress organizes Illinois as a separate territory

1818 Illinois admitted to the Union

1820 Capital moves from Kaskaskia to Vandalia

1825 Erie Canal opens, speeding up development

1832 Black Hawk's War ends resistance to white settlement

1837 Capital moves from Kaskasia to Springfield
• John Deere develops steel plow

American

1492 Christopher Columbus reaches New World

1607 Jamestown (Virginia) founded by English colonists

1620 *Mayflower* arrives at Plymouth (Massachusetts)

1754–63 French and Indian War

1765 Parliament passes Stamp Act

1775–83 Revolutionary War

1776 Signing of the Declaration of Independence

1788–90 First congressional elections

1791 Bill of Rights added to U.S. Constitution

1803 Louisiana Purchase

1812–14 War of 1812

1820 Missouri Compromise

1836 Battle of the Alamo, Texas

1846–48 Mexican-American War

1849 California Gold Rush

1860 South Carolina secedes from Union

1861–65 Civil War

1862 Lincoln signs Homestead Act

1863 Emancipation Proclamation

1865 President Lincoln assassinated (April 14)

1865–77 Reconstruction in the South

1866 Civil Rights bill passed

1881 President James Garfield shot (July 2)

History

1896 First Ford automobile is made

1898–99 Spanish-American War

1901 President William McKinley is shot (Sept. 6)

1917 U.S. enters World War I

1920 Nineteenth Amendment passed, giving women the vote

1929 U.S. stock market crash; Great Depression begins

1933 Franklin D. Roosevelt becomes president; begins New Deal

1941 Japanese attack Pearl Harbor (Dec. 7); U.S. enters World War II

1945 U.S. drops atomic bomb on Hiroshima and Nagasaki; Japan surrenders, ending World War II

1963 President Kennedy assassinated (November 22)

1964 Civil Rights Act passed

1965–73 Vietnam War

1968 Martin Luther King, Jr., shot in Memphis (April 4)

1974 President Richard Nixon resigns because of Watergate scandal

1979–81 Hostage crisis in Iran: 52 Americans held captive for 444 days

1989 End of U.S.-Soviet cold war

1991 Gulf War

1993 U.S. signs North American Free Trade Agreement with Canada and Mexico

Illinois History

1860 Abraham Lincoln elected president

1865 Lincoln is assassinated

1871 Chicago Fire leaves 300 dead and 100,000 homeless

1886 Chicago labor troubles lead to Haymarket Riot

1889 Jane Addams founds Hull-House in Chicago

1894 Federal government sends in troops to deal with the Pullman railroad strike

1917 48 die in race riots in East St. Louis

1929 Prohibition related gang violence in Chicago hits a high point in the "St. Valentine's Day Massacre"

1937 Oil is found in Marion County

1959 Opening of St. Lawrence Seaway

1968 Anti-war riots disrupt Democratic National Convention in Chicago

1973 Sears Tower, world's tallest building, completed in Chicago

1976 Richard J. Daley dies in office after 21 years as mayor of Chicago

1983 Harold Washington, Chicago's first black mayor, is elected

1980s Farm crisis leads many Illinois farmers to lose their land

1993 Mississippi floods damage millions of acres of Illinois farmland

Jean Baptiste Point du Sable (1745–1818) Born in Haiti of French and African ancestry, du Sable became a fur trader in the Mississippi Valley in the 1770s. In 1779, he founded the trading post that eventually became the city of Chicago.

Black Hawk (1767–1838) A leader of the Sauk Indian nation, Black Hawk resisted attempts to move his people from their land in Illinois. Defeated in the Black Hawk War of 1832, he died in Iowa six years later.

John Deere (1804–86) The Vermont-born mechanic invented a steel plow that was perfect for prairie soil, greatly improving farming not only in Illinois but throughout the entire Midwest.

Abraham Lincoln (1809–65) Perhaps America's greatest president, Lincoln came to Illinois at age twenty-one, later settling in Springfield, where he established a law practice and began his political career. After four years as leader of a divided nation, he was assassinated at the end of the Civil War.

Cyrus McCormick

Cyrus Hall McCormick (1809–84) Designer of the mechanical harvester, McCormick revolutionized farming in America. He built a factory in Chicago (1847) to manufacture his invention.

Stephen Arnold Douglas (1813–61) "The Little Giant" moved from Vermont to Illinois in 1833. He was elected to Congress in 1843. Douglas's successful senate campaign against Abraham Lincoln in 1858 included a series of famous debates.

Philip Danforth Armour (1832–1901) Founder of Armour & Company, Philip Armour, along with Gustavus Swift, made Chicago the nation's leading center for meat-packing in the years after the Civil War.

Marshall Field (1834–1906) One of America's greatest merchants, Field established the world's first modern department store in Chicago.

John Peter Altgeld (1847–1902) The German-born Altgeld was elected governor of Illinois in 1893. His term in office saw major social reforms.

Saint Frances Xavier Cabrini (1850–1917) Founder of the Missionary Sisters of the Sacred Heart, "Mother" Cabrini established Columbus Hospital in Chicago. In 1946 she became the first American to be canonized (made a saint).

Clarence Seward Darrow (1857–1938) Darrow moved his law practice from Ohio to Chicago in 1887. Combining a brilliant legal mind with a passion for social justice, he participated in some of the most famous trials in American history.

Jane Addams (1860–1935) Born in Cedarville, Addams worked to improve the lives of the poor in Chicago by founding Hull-House in 1889. She was co-recipient of the 1931 Nobel Prize for peace.

Frank Lloyd Wright (1867–1959) Founder of the "Prairie School" of architecture, Wright designed many distinctive structures in the Chicago area.

Carl Sandburg (1878–1967) This Galesburg native celebrated Illinois in many famous poems. He also wrote a Pulitzer Prize-winning biography of Abraham Lincoln.

Frank Lloyd Wright

Adlai Ewing Stevenson (1900–65) Grandson of a U.S. vice president, Stevenson won the Democratic presidential nomination in 1952 and 1956, losing to Dwight Eisenhower in both elections. He also served as U.S. ambassador to the United Nations (1961–65).

Enrico Fermi (1901–54) This Nobel Prize-winning physicist left fascist Italy for the U.S. in 1938. In 1942, a team of scientists led by Fermi produced the first nuclear chain reaction at the University of Chicago.

Richard Joseph Daley (1902–76) Head of the Cook County Democratic Organization, Daley was mayor of Chicago from 1955 to 1976.

Saul Bellow (b. 1915) This Montreal-born novelist moved to Chicago as a young boy and later served as a professor at the University of Chicago. He received the Nobel Prize for literature in 1976.

Gwendolyn Brooks (b. 1917) One of America's finest African-American writers, Brooks was named poet laureate of Illinois in 1968.

John Harold Johnson (b. 1918) Johnson founded Johnson Publishing Company, one of the nation's leading black-owned businesses.

Betty Friedan (b. 1921) A native of Peoria, Friedan helped launch the modern feminist movement with her book *The Feminine Mystique*. She was

Carol Moseley-Braun

a co-founder and president of the National Organization for Women.

Harold Washington (1922–87) This Chicago native served in the U.S. House of Representatives (1981–83) before becoming the city's first African-American mayor.

Jane Byrne (b. 1933) A native of Chicago, Byrne was a consumer affairs official before her election as the city's first woman mayor in 1979.

Carol Moseley-Braun (b. 1947) In 1992, after ten years as a legislator in the Illinois House of Representatives, Moseley-Braun became the first African-American woman elected to the U.S. Senate.

Pictures in this volume:

American Red Cross: 45

Associated Press/Wide World Photos: 50, 52, 53

Cahokia Mound Historical Site: 8

Chicago Architectural Photography Company: 43

Chicago Historical Society: 43, 51

Company of Military Historians: 15

Dover Pictures: 10 (both)

Fermilab Visual Media Services Office: 30

Gilcrease Institute of American Art: 14

John Hancock Mutual Insurance Company: 47

Illinois Secretary of State: 56 (both), 57 (all)

Illinois State Historical Society: 20, 24 (both)

Library of Congress: 7, 11, 12 (both), 16 (both), 17, 19 (both), 21, 22, 25, 26, 27 (both), 28, 29, 33 (both), 34, 37, 39 (both), 41, 44, 48, 49, 61

National Portrait Gallery: 60

Private Collection: p. 40

University of Chicago: 46

U.S. Senate Offices: 61

Illinois Information service: 4

About the author:

Charles A. Wills is a writer, editor, and consultant specializing in American history. He has written, edited, or contributed to more than thirty books, including many volumes in The Millbrook Press's *American Albums from the Collections of the Library of Congress* series. Wills lives in Dutchess County, New York.

Suggested reading:

Carpenter, Allen, *Enchantment of America: Illinois*, Chicago: The Childrens Press, 1963.

Howard, Robert P., *Illinois: A History of the Prairie State*. Grand Rapids, MI: Eerdmans, 1972.

Pease, Thedore Calvin. *The Story of Illinois* (3rd ed.) Chicago: The University of Chicago Press, 1965.

Stein, R. Conrad. *America the Beautiful: Illinois*, Chicago: The Childrens Press, 1987

For more information contact:

Illinois State Historical Society
Old State Capitol
Springfield, IL 62706
(217) 782-4836

Illinois Tourist Information Center
310 South Michigan Avenue
Suite 108
Chicago, IL 60604
(800) 822-0292

Page numbers in *italics* indicate illustrations